Designed and produced by
Aladdin Books Ltd
70 Old Compton Street
London W1

Design   David West
Children's Book Design
Editorial Planning   Clark Robinson Limited
Editor   Bibby Whittaker
Researcher   Cecilia Weston-Baker
Illustrated by   Ron Hayward Associates

EDITORIAL PANEL
The author, Lionel Bender, is an
author, editor and producer of
children's illustrated general science
and natural history books.

The educational consultant, Peter
Thwaites, is Head of Geography at
Windlesham House School in
Sussex.

The editorial consultant, John Clark,
has contributed to many
information and reference books.

First published in the
United States in 1988 by
Gloucester Press
387 Park Avenue South
New York, NY 10016

ISBN 0-531-17094-2

Library of Congress Catalog
Card Number: 87-82893

Printed in Belgium

PLANTS

LIONEL BENDER

GLOUCESTER PRESS
New York · London · Toronto · Sydney

12/86
Frank Watts
11.40

CONTENTS

How the book works

Each section of the book describes a group of related plants. Each begins with an introduction and a large diagram of a typical plant from the group.

Smaller diagrams explain the life cycle and the structure of the plant. Other pages have diagrams and color photographs that illustrate important points discussed in the text.

Throughout the book, charts provide a comparison of the forms and sizes of representative plants in a particular group. All illustrations are drawn to scale.

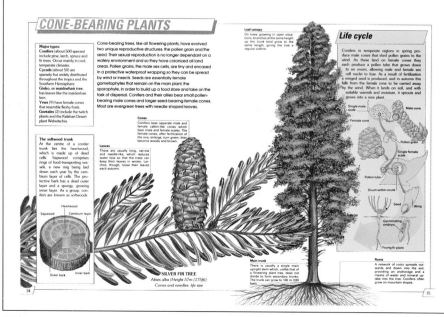

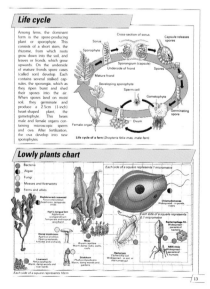

The cover photograph shows a cloud of spores shooting out of a puffball fungus.

INTRODUCTION

There are two types of living things on Earth – animals and plants. The main biological differences between the two are the ways they feed and the fact that most animals can move around whereas nearly all plants remain in one place. Animals drink water and eat plants or other animals to get the raw materials they need to function and grow. They breathe in oxygen from the air and breathe out carbon dioxide as a waste product. They also have nerves and specialized sense organs such as eyes and ears.

Plants also take in water (from the soil) but manufacture most of their own food by the process of photosynthesis. This uses the energy of sunlight to combine carbon dioxide gas from the air with water to make sugars, at the same time releasing oxygen. It is brought about by the substance chlorophyll, a pigment which is responsible for the green color of most plants. Like animals, plants are made up of cells but these have rigid walls which provide support. And unlike animals, plants have no sense organs or a nervous system. A very few plants have adapted to trap insects, which they use as a source of food and minerals.

A bee snared by an insect-eating Venus flytrap plant

PRIMITIVE PLANTS

Major types:
Bacteria are single-celled organisms, often classed as neither plant nor animal because the cell structure is simple and not all bacteria make use of photosynthesis. Single-celled true plants include pond organisms such as Euglena. These can photosynthesize but also, like animal cells, break down complex food material.
Viruses are regarded as the link between living and non-living forms.

The simplest plants consist of a single cell, with a thin skin-like covering or membrane and a complex mixture of chemicals inside. Among these chemicals is chlorophyll, a green pigment that can trap the energy of sunlight and use it to power chemical reactions within the cell. Some bacteria are single-celled organisms of this type. Other primitive plants, such as water plants that resemble bundles of green hair, are made up of thread-like chains of cells. Next on the scale of complexity are seaweeds and mosses, which also have simple chains of cells in their multicellular bodies. Groups of specially modified cells carry the plants' reproductive organs. At a slightly higher level still are ferns, which grow leafy fronds. The fronds have areas on their undersides which carry spores, from which the plants reproduce.

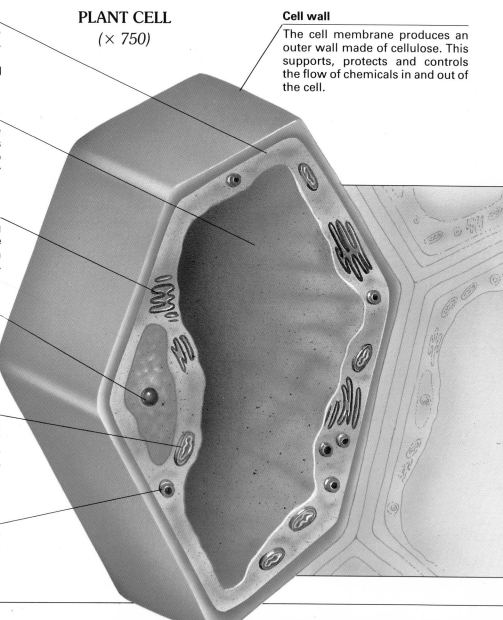

PLANT CELL
(× 750)

Membrane and cytoplasm

A thin membrane encloses the jelly-like contents of the cell (cytoplasm), in which are embedded all the working parts of the cell called the organelles.

Vacuole

At the center of the cell is a space filled with water, the vacuole. This enlarges as the plant takes up water, and gets smaller in dry conditions.

Endoplasmic reticulum

This system of fine tubes running through the cytoplasm allows the movement of chemicals between the nucleus and the cell membrane.

Nucleus

The control center of the cell. It is enclosed within a membrane and contains the genetic material that directs the cell's actions.

Mitochondrion

One of many energy-producing centers within the cytoplasm. Mitochondria are usually oval-shaped and are often called the cell's powerhouses.

Chloroplast

Similar to mitochondria, chloroplasts contain the green pigment chlorophyll, which traps the energy of sunlight to make sugars.

Cell wall

The cell membrane produces an outer wall made of cellulose. This supports, protects and controls the flow of chemicals in and out of the cell.

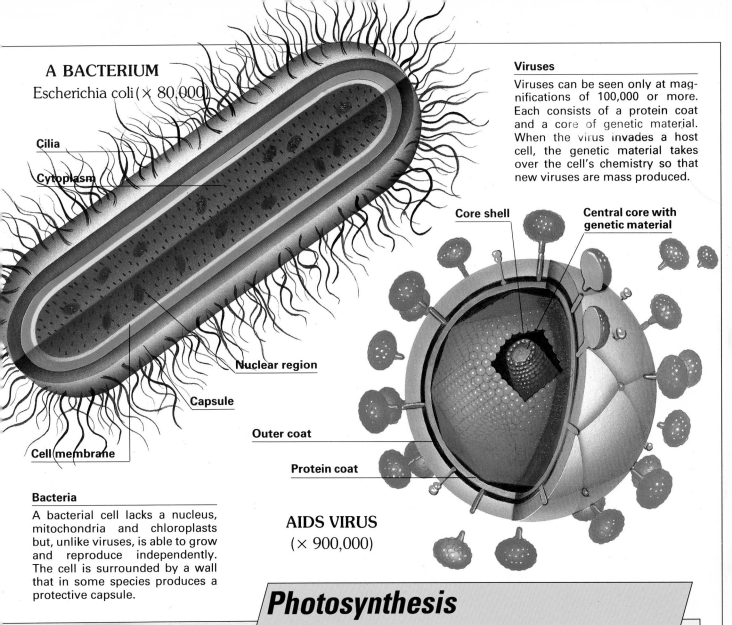

A BACTERIUM
Escherichia coli (× 80,000)

- Cilia
- Cytoplasm
- Nuclear region
- Capsule
- Cell membrane

Viruses
Viruses can be seen only at magnifications of 100,000 or more. Each consists of a protein coat and a core of genetic material. When the virus invades a host cell, the genetic material takes over the cell's chemistry so that new viruses are mass produced.

- Core shell
- Central core with genetic material
- Outer coat
- Protein coat

AIDS VIRUS
(× 900,000)

Bacteria
A bacterial cell lacks a nucleus, mitochondria and chloroplasts but, unlike viruses, is able to grow and reproduce independently. The cell is surrounded by a wall that in some species produces a protective capsule.

Photosynthesis

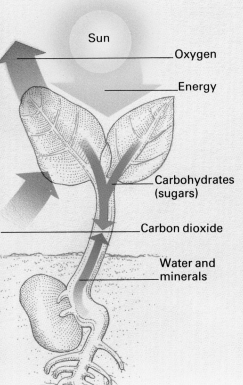

- Sun
- Oxygen
- Energy
- Carbohydrates (sugars)
- Carbon dioxide
- Water and minerals

Cells cannot live without energy, food, water and oxygen. Animal cells feed on plant or animal material and break down the large, complex chemicals within this to obtain essential nutrients and energy. Oxygen and water pass into the cells from the surroundings. Plant cells, by contrast, use the energy of sunlight to convert carbon dioxide and water into sugars, which is the function of photosynthesis. They then convert the sugars into other nutrients or break them down to release energy. A typical flowering plant, from a grass to an oak tree, takes up water and mineral salts from the soil through its roots. Carbon dioxide enters the leaves through tiny holes in the leaf surface. In sunlight, sugars are made and oxygen is formed, which then passes out of the plant's leaves. At night, the plant uses oxygen to break down the sugars.

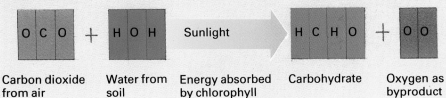

| O C O | + | H O H | Sunlight | → | H C H O | + | O O |

Carbon dioxide from air — Water from soil — Energy absorbed by chlorophyll — Carbohydrate — Oxygen as byproduct

ALGAE

There are about 20,000 species of algae, found in fresh water and seas throughout the world. They include green algae, such as the common hair-like pond plant called Spirogyra and the "leafy" sea lettuce Ulva, and the red and brown algae, common as seashore seaweeds such as bladderwrack, oar weed and dulse.

Algae range in size and form from microscopic single-celled plants that live on damp rocks or corals to the multicellular 60 m (200 feet) long strap-like seaweeds such as kelp, which are found off the coasts of California. They contain one or more types of pigment and obtain energy by photosynthesis. They are simple in structure. Blue-green algae are microscopic plants that resemble bacteria, and even the largest of seaweeds lack distinct roots, stems and leaves. Most algae are aquatic and are found in ponds, lakes and seas, where they sometimes multiply so rapidly that they color the water green or – in species with a red pigment – pink or orange.

Single or in groups

Two types of single-celled algae-like species are the diatoms and desmids. Diatoms have shell-like cases made of silica, the chemical of sand, and consist of two sections. Some diatoms are circular and resemble a hat box with a base and a lid. Others are sausage-, oval- or S-shaped. Desmids also have a cell in two sections, but instead of a silica shell have a cellulose cell wall, as in more complex plants. The pond alga Spirogyra is made up of a string, or filament, of identical cells. Among seaweeds, the common feathery green and red types consist of highly branched filaments joined together, whereas kelps are composed of various types of cells arranged in groups to form leaf-like fronds.

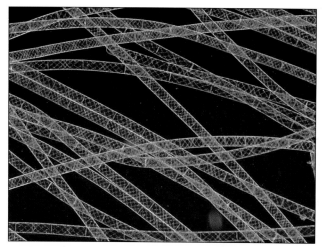
Spirogyra consists of hair-like filaments.

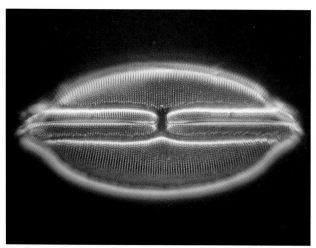
A diatom enlarged 2,000 times

Green, brown and red seaweeds at low tide

Reproduction

Some microscopic seaweeds are able to reproduce by breaking up into parts. Blue-green algae and some single-celled green algae reproduce by forming buds that split off or by growth and division of the cell in two. Colonies of such species as Volvox result from repeated cell divisions and are held together by a slimy sheath. The freshwater and seawater green alga called Chlamydomonas can reproduce both sexually and asexually. A single cell can divide into two identical daughter cells (asexually) or, as shown below, give rise to the equivalent of male and female sex cells, or gametes. Gametes from different plants fuse to form first a zygote and then a zygospore, which has a thick protective cell wall. The zygospore later germinates into four new cells.

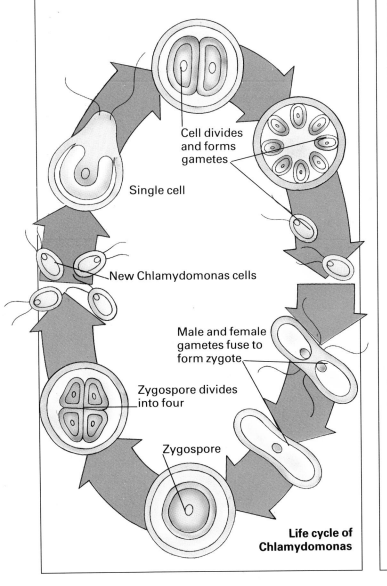

Cell divides and forms gametes

Single cell

New Chlamydomonas cells

Male and female gametes fuse to form zygote

Zygospore divides into four

Zygospore

Life cycle of Chlamydomonas

Life style

Large seaweeds of the seashore and coastal waters are usually attached to rocks by means of a flat plate-like base, the holdfast. Their long, flat fronds wave about in the water currents. In spring, swellings appear on the tips of fronds and shed male and female gametes into the water. The gametes fuse and produce zygospores that later develop into new plants. Blue-green and other single-celled algae are found in most damp, warm habitats where there is adequate light. Some live inside flatworms that burrow in sand as the tide comes in and move to the surface as the tide ebbs. The algae provide the worms with food in the form of sugars made by photosynthesis. The algae need sunlight for this, which is provided as the flatworms migrate to the surface when there is no danger.

Kelp is one of the largest seaweeds.

Flatworms colored green by the algae

FUNGI

Fungi are often classified separately from other plants because they lack chlorophyll and most have a simple cell structure. Many live as parasites, dissolving dead or decaying animal and plant matter and feeding on the nutrient-rich liquid. There are more than 100,000 species of fungi, ranging from single-celled yeasts to multicellular mushrooms and toadstools. Fungi inhabit nearly every environment where life is possible. They are chief enemies of larger plants and some cause human diseases – for example, ringworm. However, some molds produce chemicals used as antibiotic drugs. And yeasts make bread dough rise and bring about the fermentation used to make alcohol in wine and beer.

Structure

Yeasts are single cells that are often enclosed in a slimy capsule, and have a well-defined nucleus and a cell wall made of various sugars. Another group of fungi, the molds, rusts and smuts, are made up of a network of narrow tubular branches called hyphae. These are the feeding structures common to all large fungi. Hyphae consist of yeast-like cells fused together to form a hollow cylinder. In toadstools and mushrooms the network of hyphae is underground. At the tips of mature hyphae are the toadstools and mushrooms as we see them. These reproductive structures or sporangia produce spores.

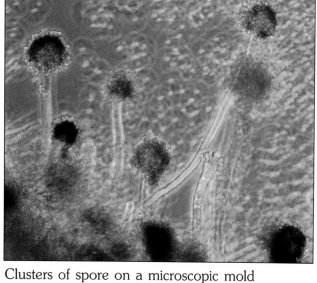

Clusters of spore on a microscopic mold

Spores

Sporangium

Developing sporangium

Network of hyphae

Nuclei

Hypha wall

Vacuole (empty space)

Cutaway section of single hypha

Feeding

The common bread mold and similar fungi live on rotting vegetation or on fruit. They produce hair-like hyphae that penetrate the food source in the same way that the roots of other plants spread through the soil. Cells of the hyphae release chemicals known as enzymes. These break down complex substances such as proteins, fats and sugars into simpler ones which, along with water and vital mineral salts, readily pass into the hyphae.

A bracket fungus growing on a tree trunk

Reproduction

Most fungi reproduce by forming spores. When a spore lands on a suitable material it sprouts, producing a network of hyphae. This produces fruiting bodies (sporangia) which, in mushrooms and toadstools, consists of an "umbrella" with gills densely covered with spore-producing structures. The spores are shot out of the gills and carried away by the wind. Stinkhorns produce spores that are dispersed when they stick to the bodies of insects, such as flies.

A puffball releasing a cloud of spores

Partnerships

Lichens are primitive plants formed by the partnership of a fungus and an alga. The fungus makes up the main body of the plant, providing a home for groups of cells of the alga. In return, the alga uses photosynthesis to make sugars that the fungus absorbs as food. The combined organism grows more slowly and is more resilient and adaptable than either partner. There are more than 15,000 species of lichen. They are found on rocks, buildings and tree trunks, and range in size from that of a pinhead to leafy structures 2m (7ft) across. Some produce antibiotic drugs effective against diseases such as pneumonia. One, Cladonia rangiferina, is called reindeer moss because it is the main food of reindeer during the Arctic winter, when there is little other plant food.

Reindeer feeding on reindeer moss (a lichen)

MOSSES AND LIVERWORTS

Mosses: about 14,000 species including the bog mosses Sphagnum. **Liverworts:** 9,000 species, each with a flattened appearance. **Hornworts:** about 100 species that resemble liverworts but have a different type of spore-producing capsule.

Growing as a blanket-like covering on ponds, river banks and the floors of damp woods, or as the mat of vegetation forming bogs, mosses and liverworts are the simplest and most primitive of land plants. Although similar to seaweeds, with a compact body many cells thick and a method of sexual reproduction dependent on water, their cell structure is like that of more highly evolved plants with an outer layer (the epidermis) that prevents them from drying out. Most mosses, liverworts and the related hornworts are small green plants. They grow best in warm moist climates and most species are found in the tropics, growing on tree trunks or on the forest floor.

Life cycle

As an adaptation to living on land, mosses and liverworts have a complex life cycle involving two distinct stages. The first and main stage, called the gametophyte, depends on water for reproduction. The second stage, the sporophyte, produces microscopic spores that can survive periods of drought before germinating.

The gametophyte reproduces sexually, producing male and female organs called the antheridium and archegonium. In mosses especially, these organs can be seen developing at the tips of the upright growing leaf shoots. They produce sex cells, or gametes: male spermatozoids and female ova. The spermatozoids must swim to the ova to fertilize them and, because the male and female organs may be on separate plants, this requires the surface of the plants to be covered in water. On land this occurs along river banks, when it rains or when there is a heavy dew. The fertilized ova develop into spore-producing forms, the sporophytes. These grow as parasites on the mature plant, absorbing food from its leaves. They send up an aerial shoot with a capsule at the tip that produces thousands of spores. The spores are carried away by the wind. When they reach a suitable habitat, each spore sprouts and forms a young shoot, called the protonema. This develops underground roots and an aerial shoot, and eventually forms a new gametophyte plant.

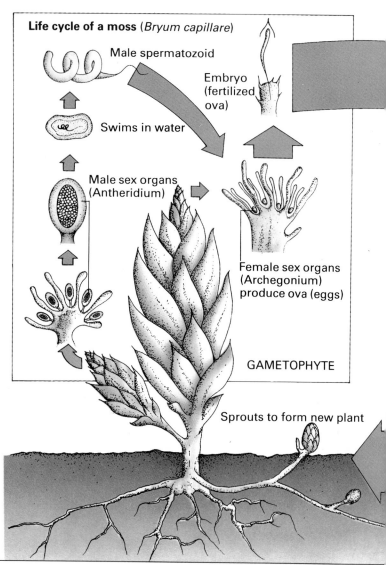

Life cycle of a moss (*Bryum capillare*)

Male spermatozoid

Embryo (fertilized ova)

Swims in water

Male sex organs (Antheridium)

Female sex organs (Archegonium) produce ova (eggs)

GAMETOPHYTE

Sprouts to form new plant

Star-shaped female sex organs of a liverwort

The main body of common liverworts such as Marchantia and Conocephalum, which grow on river banks throughout the world, and of hornworts, is a plate-like structure often resembling the lobes of a liver. This is why (and because they were once used to treat diseases of the liver) they are called liverworts. Leafy liverworts, such as Pleurozia in peat bogs, have branched creeping stems clothed with tiny leaves. Mosses have a similar form but the stems grow more upright and the leaves are largely made up of hollow cells with small pores in their walls so that they absorb and store large amounts of water. Mosses such as Sphagnum grow in dense masses, their lower parts decaying slowly to form peat.

A close-up of Sphagnum moss

Sporophyte grows on gametophyte plant

Capsule

SPOROPHYTE

Spores blown by wind

Protonema

Lobed "leaves" of the great scented liverwort

11

FERNS

Ferns (about 100,000 species) produce spores in stalked spore cases that grow in clusters under mature leaves. Horsetails (30) produce spores in cones and manufacture most food in their ridged stem. Clubmosses (1,250) are small and moss-like and produce spores in club-like cones. All three types grow in greatest numbers and diversity in rain forests of Southeast Asia.

Ferns are leafy plants which, in complexity, lie between primitive and highly evolved plants. Like algae, mosses and liverworts they have a life cycle with two forms, are spread by spores, and are dependent on water for male sex cells to swim to the female cells. But like cone- and seed-bearing plants, they have a main body divided into roots, stems and leaves and a network of tubes, the vascular system, that links these and permits movement of food and water to all parts of the plant. Horsetails and clubmosses resemble ferns in structure and partly in life style, but their leaves are minute and scale-like and the spore-bearing tissues are grouped into cones.

Structure

Horsetails have an upright stem, sprays of green branches and small scale-like leaves. Clubmosses usually have tufts of branching stems covered with tiny leaves. Ferns grow as shrubs, creeping vine-like plants, or even as trees. All three types have a vascular system in which elongated cells are grouped and linked together to form either parallel columns or a meshwork (lattice) of conducting tissue. The vascular system extends from the tips of water-absorbing roots into the food-producing leaves. In ferns especially, the cells of the system are rigid and provide support for the plants.

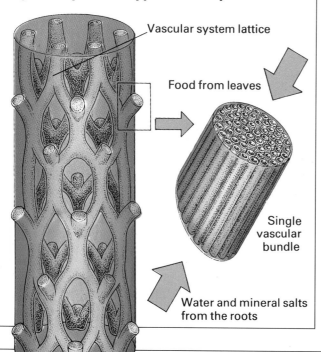

Vascular system lattice

Food from leaves

Single vascular bundle

Water and mineral salts from the roots

Shape and form

Roots anchor ferns to the soil, allowing them to grow upright stems bearing many leaves, and some ferns reach tree-like proportions. True tree ferns are tropical species with trunks built up of leaf bases, as in palm trees. They can grow to 21m (70ft) tall. Bracken is a fern often regarded as a weed because it thrives on pasture land. Horsetails vary from small creeping plants to scramblers reaching 9m (30ft) across. Clubmosses once included giant tree forms that were buried in bogs millions of years ago and formed into coal, but most present-day species are only small plants.

Spore-bearing cones of a horsetail

Life cycle

Among ferns, the dominant form is the spore-producing plant or sporophyte. This consists of a short stem, the rhizome, from which roots grow down into the soil, and leaves or fronds, which grow upward. On the underside of mature fronds spore cases (called sori) develop. Each contains several stalked capsules, the sporangia, which as they ripen burst and shed their spores into the air. When spores land on moist soil, they germinate and produce a 2.5cm (1-inch) heart-shaped plant, the gametophyte. This bears male and female organs containing microscopic sperm and ova. After fertilization, the ova develop into new sporophytes.

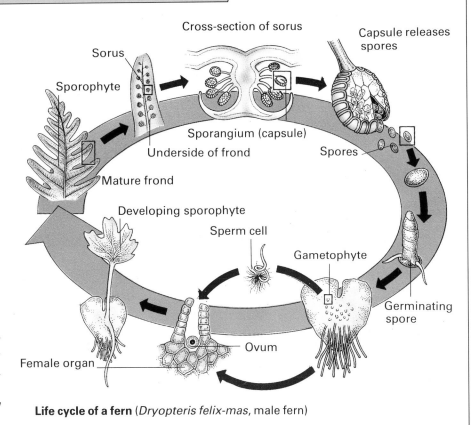

Life cycle of a fern (*Dryopteris felix-mas*, male fern)

Lower plants chart

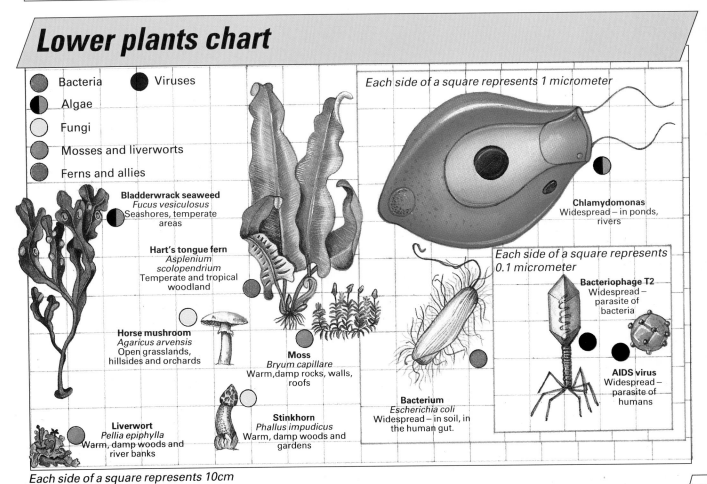

Bacteria   Viruses

Algae

Fungi

Mosses and liverworts

Ferns and allies

Each side of a square represents 1 micrometer

Bladderwrack seaweed
Fucus vesiculosus
Seashores, temperate areas

Chlamydomonas
Widespread – in ponds, rivers

Hart's tongue fern
Asplenium scolopendrium
Temperate and tropical woodland

Each side of a square represents 0.1 micrometer

Bacteriophage T2
Widespread – parasite of bacteria

Horse mushroom
Agaricus arvensis
Open grasslands, hillsides and orchards

Moss
Bryum capillare
Warm, damp rocks, walls, roofs

AIDS virus
Widespread – parasite of humans

Bacterium
Escherichia coli
Widespread – in soil, in the human gut.

Liverwort
Pellia epiphylla
Warm, damp woods and river banks

Stinkhorn
Phallus impudicus
Warm, damp woods and gardens

Each side of a square represents 10cm

13

CONE-BEARING PLANTS

Major types:

Conifers (about 500 species) include pine, larch, spruce and fir trees. Occur mainly in cool, temperate climates.

Cycads (about 50) are sparsely but widely distributed throughout the tropics and the Southern Hemisphere.

Ginkgo, or maidenhair tree, has leaves like the maidenhair fern.

Yews (9) have female cones that resemble fleshy fruits.

Gnetales (2) include the twitch plants and the Kalahari Desert plant Welwitschia.

Cone-bearing trees, like all flowering plants, have evolved two unique reproductive structures: the pollen grain and the seed. Their sexual reproduction is no longer dependent on a watery environment and so they have colonized all land areas. Pollen grains, the male sex cells, are tiny and encased in a protective waterproof wrapping so they can be spread by wind or insects. Seeds are essentially female gametophytes that remain on the main plant, the sporophyte, in order to build up a food store and take on the task of dispersal. Conifers and their allies bear small pollen-bearing male cones and larger seed-bearing female cones. Most are evergreen trees with needle-shaped leaves.

Cones

Conifers bear separate male and female catkin-like cones which bear male and female scales. The female cones, after fertilization of the ova, enlarge, turn green, then become woody and brown.

The softwood trunk

At the center of a conifer trunk lies the heartwood, which is made up of dead cells. Sapwood comprises rings of food-transporting vessels, a new ring being laid down each year by the cambium layer of cells. The protective bark has a dead outer layer and a spongy, growing inner layer. As a group, conifers are known as softwoods.

Leaves

These are usually long, narrow and needle-like, which reduces water loss so that the trees can keep their leaves in winter. Larches, though, lose their leaves each autumn.

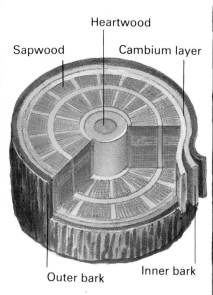

Heartwood

Sapwood   Cambium layer

Outer bark   Inner bark

SILVER FIR TREE
Abies alba (Height 57m [175ft])
Cones and needles: life size

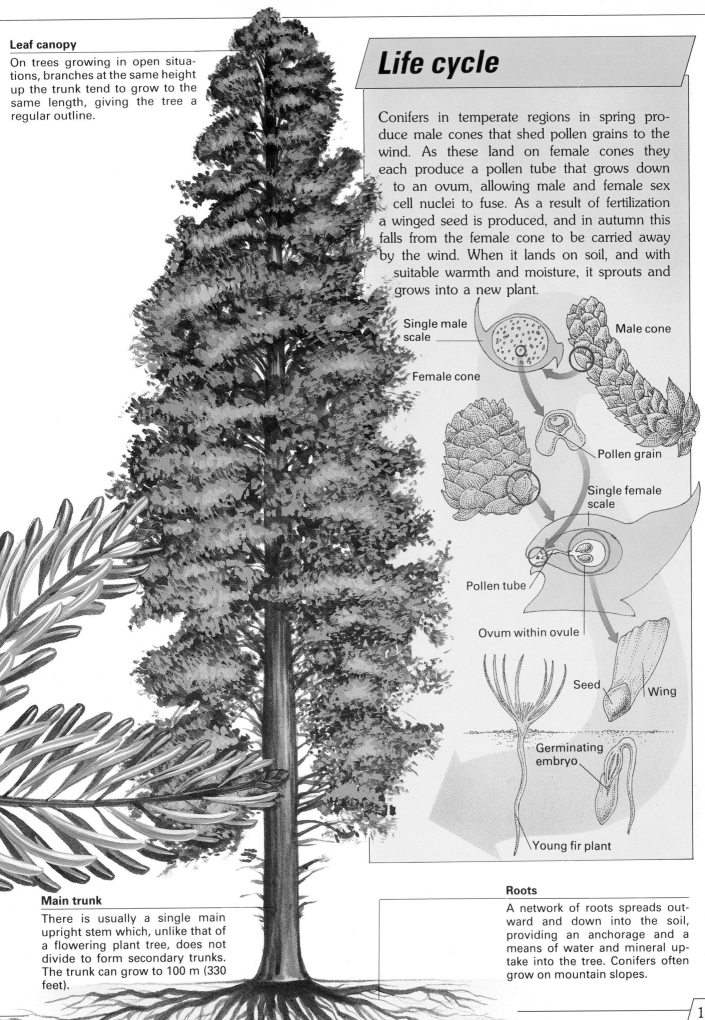

Leaf canopy

On trees growing in open situations, branches at the same height up the trunk tend to grow to the same length, giving the tree a regular outline.

Life cycle

Conifers in temperate regions in spring produce male cones that shed pollen grains to the wind. As these land on female cones they each produce a pollen tube that grows down to an ovum, allowing male and female sex cell nuclei to fuse. As a result of fertilization a winged seed is produced, and in autumn this falls from the female cone to be carried away by the wind. When it lands on soil, and with suitable warmth and moisture, it sprouts and grows into a new plant.

Single male scale

Male cone

Female cone

Pollen grain

Single female scale

Pollen tube

Ovum within ovule

Seed

Wing

Germinating embryo

Young fir plant

Main trunk

There is usually a single main upright stem which, unlike that of a flowering plant tree, does not divide to form secondary trunks. The trunk can grow to 100 m (330 feet).

Roots

A network of roots spreads outward and down into the soil, providing an anchorage and a means of water and mineral uptake into the tree. Conifers often grow on mountain slopes.

Trunk

About 230 million years ago conifer trees dominated the Earth's plants, forming a thick belt of forest over much of the land. Today relatively few types remain, but of these the North American Douglas fir, giant sequoia and California redwoods are the tallest trees in the world, standing up to 115m (385 feet) tall and with a distance around the base of the trunk of 14m (46 feet). Yews are among the slowest growing trees. Plants in the Arctic regions along the edge of the forest belt can take tens of years to grow just a few inches in height. The trunk wood of conifers is soft and contains chemicals known as resins. These give freshly cut softwood a characteristic smell of turpentine. In cross-section the wood differs from that of flowering plant trees in that lengthwise water-containing vessels are absent. In the north of America, Europe and Asia conifer trees are often grown in huge plantations as a source of commercial wood. When the trees are fully grown they are cut down and transported to lumberyards. Here the softwood is used as timber for building, or to make plywood or chipboard.

Logs can be burned as fuel.

Sequoia, the world's largest tree

Leaves

Fir trees bear evergreen leaves or needles in groups of two to five at regular intervals along the stems. Larches have deciduous leaves or needles similarly arranged but in clusters of ten or more. Cypress trees are Northern Hemisphere conifers with evergreen scale-like leaves pressed closely against the stems. Pine trees are the most familiar conifer in North America.

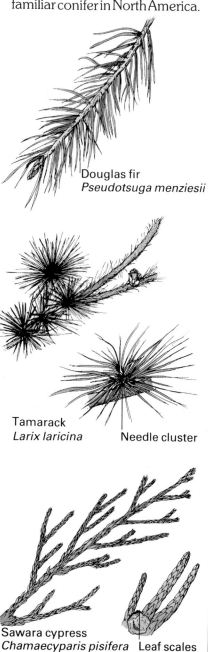

Douglas fir
Pseudotsuga menziesii

Tamarack
Larix laricina   Needle cluster

Sawara cypress
Chamaecyparis pisifera   Leaf scales

Cones

Conifers are often called gymnosperms (meaning naked seeds) because the ovules — ova-containing structures — are borne directly on special leaves, the scales, and not enclosed in an ovary as in flowering plants. The scales are grouped together to form cones. Cones are either male or female. In many species the sexes are on different trees, but in the larger conifers there are often male and female cones on the same shoots. Yews produce single ovules not on scales like true conifers but surrounded by a fleshy berry-like aril. The cones of cycads can grow to 60 cm (2 feet) and weigh 25 kg (55 lb).

The cone of a rare cycad

"Cones" of yews look like berries.

Cone-bearing plants chart

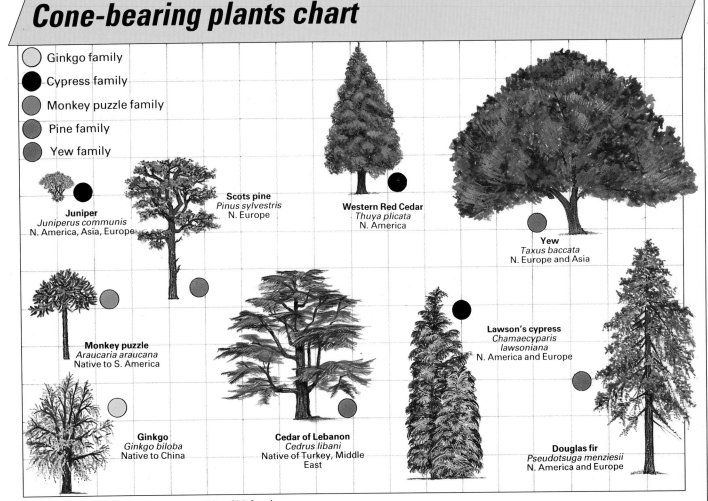

- ○ Ginkgo family
- ● Cypress family
- ◉ Monkey puzzle family
- ◉ Pine family
- ◉ Yew family

Juniper
Juniperus communis
N. America, Asia, Europe

Scots pine
Pinus sylvestris
N. Europe

Western Red Cedar
Thuya plicata
N. America

Yew
Taxus baccata
N. Europe and Asia

Monkey puzzle
Araucaria araucana
Native to S. America

Cedar of Lebanon
Cedrus libani
Native of Turkey, Middle East

Lawson's cypress
Chamaecyparis lawsoniana
N. America and Europe

Ginkgo
Ginkgo biloba
Native to China

Douglas fir
Pseudotsuga menziesii
N. America and Europe

Each side of a square represents 10m (30 feet)

FLOWERING PLANTS

Two main types:
Monocots have only one leaf-like organ, or cotyledon, within the seed. They include grasses, palms and orchids (55,000 species). They have narrow leaves and the petals of the flowers arranged in threes or sixes. **Dicots** have two cotyledons within the seed. They include woody trees and shrubs and many plants grown for food and garden decoration (200,000 species). They have a variety of leaf shapes and flowers with petals usually arranged in fours or fives.

More than 80 per cent of all living green plants – some 255,000 species – are flowering plants. They are the dominant group of land plants in the world today and include most trees, all grasses, herbs, carnivorous plants and many aquatic plants. They differ from other seed-bearing plants such as conifers in usually having flowers, seeds enclosed in fruits, and a well-developed food- and water-conducting system. Flowers bear pollen-producing male organs and egg cells that form the female ovule. They encourage transfer of pollen from flower to flower – pollination – by insects and other animals. Flowering plants are also known as angiosperms (meaning covered seeds). This refers to a layer of tissue called the carpel, which encloses the seed and later forms a fruit which aids the seed's dispersal.

Life cycle

Flowers are concerned with sexual reproduction. The male parts are the stamens, and the female parts consist of a pollen-receiving stigma and an ovary, which bears the embryo seed or ovule. Pollen grains are carried to the stigma by the wind or by insects such as bees and flies. There the pollen grain produces a pollen tube that penetrates the ovule. Pollen and ovule cell nuclei fuse and produce an embryo. As the embryo develops, the carpel forms a food store, the endosperm, and a seed coat, the testa. The seed ripens and the stamens, petals and sepals fall off to leave a fruit. The fruit is carried by the wind or by an animal. Given warmth and moisture, the seed germinates to produce first a small root, then a leaf shoot. The cotyledons provide food for the young plant and protect the first true leaves.

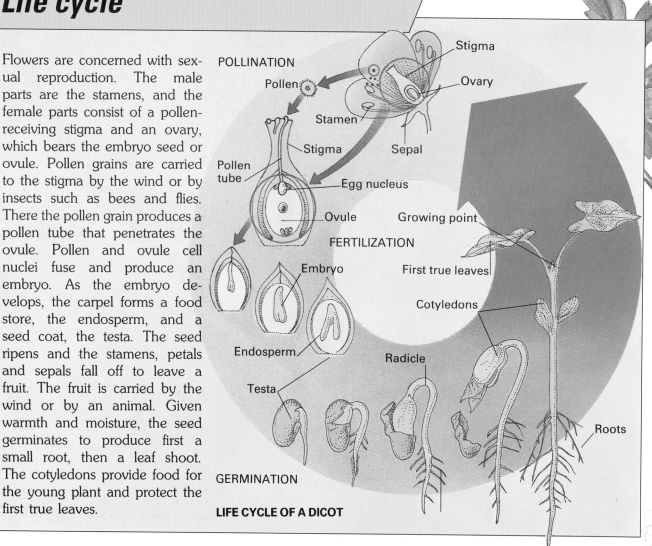

LIFE CYCLE OF A DICOT

MEADOW BUTTERCUP
Ranunculus acris

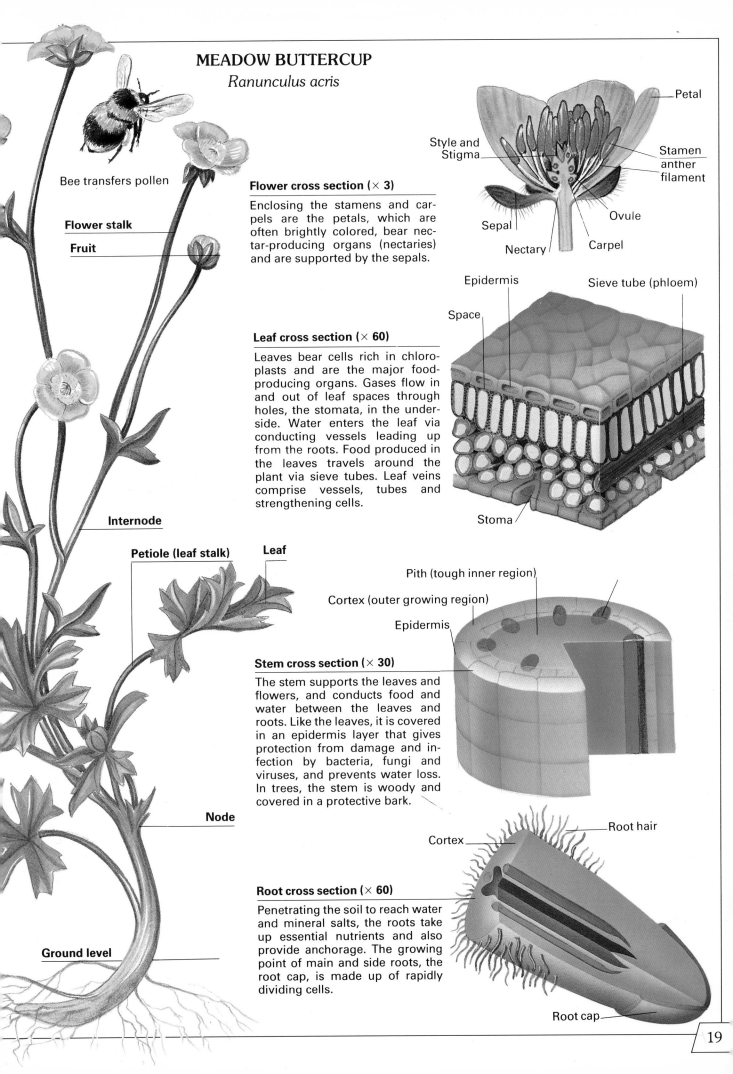

Bee transfers pollen

Flower stalk

Fruit

Internode

Petiole (leaf stalk)   **Leaf**

Node

Ground level

Flower cross section (× 3)

Enclosing the stamens and carpels are the petals, which are often brightly colored, bear nectar-producing organs (nectaries) and are supported by the sepals.

Style and Stigma

Petal

Stamen
anther
filament

Sepal

Ovule

Nectary

Carpel

Leaf cross section (× 60)

Leaves bear cells rich in chloroplasts and are the major food-producing organs. Gases flow in and out of leaf spaces through holes, the stomata, in the underside. Water enters the leaf via conducting vessels leading up from the roots. Food produced in the leaves travels around the plant via sieve tubes. Leaf veins comprise vessels, tubes and strengthening cells.

Epidermis

Sieve tube (phloem)

Space

Stoma

Stem cross section (× 30)

The stem supports the leaves and flowers, and conducts food and water between the leaves and roots. Like the leaves, it is covered in an epidermis layer that gives protection from damage and infection by bacteria, fungi and viruses, and prevents water loss. In trees, the stem is woody and covered in a protective bark.

Pith (tough inner region)

Cortex (outer growing region)

Epidermis

Root hair

Cortex

Root cross section (× 60)

Penetrating the soil to reach water and mineral salts, the roots take up essential nutrients and also provide anchorage. The growing point of main and side roots, the root cap, is made up of rapidly dividing cells.

Root cap

TREES AND SHRUBS (Temperate)

The term shrub is used for woody plants that lack an obvious trunk but have a number of shoots rising up from the base. Temperate shrubs include hawthorn, hazel and birch. Temperate deciduous forest trees include oak, ash, beech and elm.

Temperate regions include much of North America, northern Eurasia and coastal regions of Australasia.

In temperate regions the climate tends to be warm or hot in summer and cold in winter. The marked cold season limits the type of flowering plants that can grow in these areas. Most trees that grow there shed their leaves in autumn to cope with the limited supply of water during the winter and to avoid frost damage. Within any one species, trees that grow in very cold areas – where conifers usually dominate – tend to be shorter and more shrub-like than those growing in warmer parts. The flowers of temperate trees and shrubs are mostly small and inconspicuous and are usually adapted for wind or wind and insect pollination, because there are fewer insects there than in the tropics.

Leaves and fruits

In spring, temperate trees and shrubs put on a growth spurt and develop new leaves and flowers. Throughout spring and summer the leaves photosynthesize and build up the plant's food reserves. A considerable amount of nutrients and energy is used to form seeds that will disperse the plant and to develop leaf buds for next year's growth. In autumn, deciduous trees shed all their leaves. Evergreen trees and shrubs, such as holly, shed their leaves in small numbers throughout the year. Cells at the base of the leaf stalk form a corky layer which stops the flow of water to the leaf. Eventually the leaf dies and falls off.

Holly is an evergreen shrub.

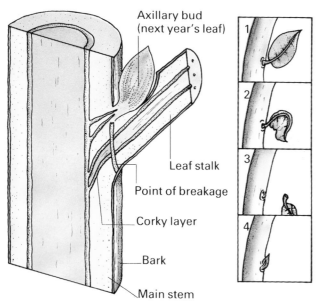

Axillary bud
(next year's leaf)

Leaf stalk

Point of breakage

Corky layer

Bark

Main stem

1
2
3
4

Acorns are the fruits of the oak tree.

Pollination

The transfer of pollen from male anthers to female stigma is called pollination. Catkins, the clusters of tiny flowers of trees such as hazel, use the wind for pollination. They are borne on stems before the leaves appear. Each flower produces a mass of light pollen grains that are easily shaken off by the slightest breeze. The stigma sticks out beyond the petals to catch any pollen that blows by. Most fruit trees, such as apples, have scented flowers that are attractive to insects. As an insect feeds on the pollen or nectar, it brushes against the anthers and pollen sticks to its hairs. When the insect visits another flower, the pollen brushes off on the stigma.

Pollen showers from hazel catkins

A bee transfers pollen on cherry blossom.

Yearly cycle

Deciduous trees, such as oak, horse chestnut and ash, change their appearance with the seasons. At the beginning of spring, branches and twigs are bare of leaves and flowers. By summer the tree is in full leaf and flowers have appeared. After pollination, seeds and fruits develop. With the onset of autumn, the leaves start to turn color and fall, and the fruits begin to be dispersed or are eaten by animals such as squirrels and birds. During winter, the tree is almost dormant. Buds are the only visible signs of life, but they do not open until spring. Many trees can live several hundred years, repeating this growth pattern with the endless cycle of the seasons.

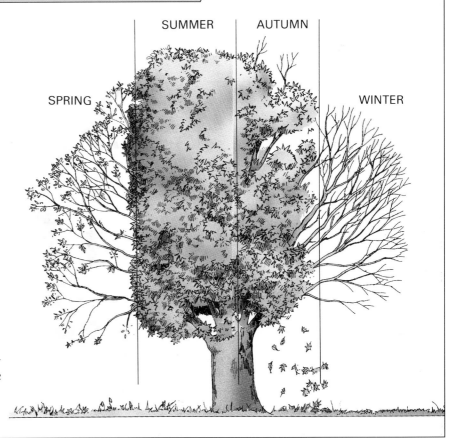

SUMMER   AUTUMN

SPRING   WINTER

TREES AND SHRUBS (Tropical)

There are two major types: **Food trees and shrubs** – species that produce leaves and fruits that are used for drinks and food – for example tea, coffee, cocoa, banana and date palm. **Timber trees and shrubs** – species that produce a tough wood, such as mahogany, teak and ebony.

The tropics – the world's perpetually hot climates – include most of central Africa, southern Asia, northern Australasia and northern South America. In the hottest and wettest regions, such as the Amazon River basin, many kinds of evergreen flowering plants thrive. The trees have a year-long growing season and form thick, lush rainforests, often called jungle. Where there is less rainfall and a distinct dry season each year, both deciduous and semi-evergreen trees grow. At the fringes of the tropics the dry season may last for many months. There most of the trees are deciduous and, like the acacias of the African savannah, are mostly flat-topped and widely scattered.

Shapes and sizes

Tropical rainforests contain the greatest diversity and number of flowering trees and shrubs. There are five zones of vegetation. The tallest trees grow to 60 m (200 feet) and produce a mass of branches, leaves and flowers – the crown – at the top of their trunk. The crowns stick up high above the rest of the forest, receiving the maximum of light. Below is the canopy, or forest roof, an interlocking mass of crowns of trees 15-30 m (50-100 ft) tall. Scattered below are trees up to 15 m (50 ft) tall with crowns shaped by the direction of light. At the lowest level are young trees and shrubs.

Tall trees that thrust their crowns high above the forest roof are known as emergents.

Broad crowns of closely packed trees form an almost unbroken sea of foliage 30 m (100 ft) above the forest floor.

Beneath the canopy trees compete for light. Their tops seem to stretch up in search of sunlight.

Sparse shrubs and young trees grow in the shadowy gloom of the other trees.

Ferns grow on the damp forest soil.

Tall trees in the Venezuelan rainforest

Trunk and leaves

With many tall tropical trees, the base of the trunk and roots form thick supporting buttresses. Higher up, the trunk and branches act as hosts for other flowering plants such as strangler figs. These grow from seeds that lodge in the host's bark and send down roots that surround and gradually decompose it. Trees of dry areas of the tropics, such as the baobab of Africa, have a small crown and a trunk that stores water to allow the plant to survive long periods of drought. The eucalyptus, or gum, trees of Australia produce evergreen water-retaining leaves of two types – rounded, stalkless young leaves and small, long and narrow, stalked adult ones.

A fat-trunked baobab tree in Kenya

Koalas feed on Australian eucalyptus trees.

Fruits

With constant sunshine and rain, tropical trees and shrubs can produce fruit all year round. The fruits are often large and colorful and have juicy, tasty centers – such as with bananas and mangos. This encourages animals to feed on them, and in this way the animals disperse the seeds that are inside the fruits. Many fruits of emergent trees are eaten by birds such as toucans and hornbills. Those of forest canopy trees form the diet of monkeys and apes, which are constantly on the move in search of trees in fruit. Trees that grow by the water's edge, such as coconut palms of tropical island beaches, produce fruits that can withstand salt water and float on the currents. Mangrove swamp trees form fruits that do not rot when submerged in water.

Bananas are a favorite food of spider monkeys

A young coconut palm sprouting on a beach

HERBACEOUS PLANTS (Bulbs, corms)

Major types:
Bulbs are fat, rounded organs with fleshy food-filled leaves, as in daffodils and snowdrops. **Corms** are rounded, squat, swollen stems produced by crocuses, for example. **Tubers** are fat, oval underground stems with tiny leaves and buds, as in potatoes. **Rhizomes** are long, swollen stems with a bud at one end, as in many grasses and irises.

Bulbs and corms – and the related rhizomes and tubers – are underground food-storage organs of soft-stemmed, or herbaceous, plants that grow from year to year. Such long-lived plants are known as perennials. Trees and shrubs are woody perennials and even in the coldest regions their trunks and branches persist all year round. By contrast, in winter herbaceous perennials either keep some leaves and slow down their growth, as with grasses, or lose all their leaves and remain as a dormant underground form, as with onions and tulips. In both cases, the part that remains underground acts as storage for food which is used for new growth the next spring.

Annual cycle

Plants that produce bulbs, corms and tubers reproduce in two ways, asexually and sexually. The asexual method is often known as vegetative propagation. It involves shoots formed from side buds that develop into roots and leaves, and eventually separate from the parent plant. No flowers, pollination or fertilization of ovules are involved. In daffodils, for example, in the spring an overwintering bulb produces leaves and a flower stalk. While the flower blossoms and its seeds set, the leaves send food down to a developing side bud which by the end of the growing season has formed a daughter bulb. Vegetative propagation produces clumps of plants which, because of their underground food storage and buds, are resistant to damage and disease.

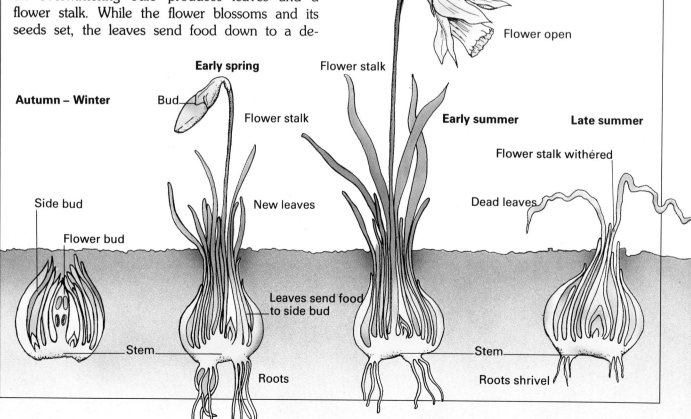

Autumn – Winter — Side bud — Flower bud — Stem — Roots

Early spring — Bud — Flower stalk — New leaves — Leaves send food to side bud

Flower open — Flower stalk

Early summer

Late summer — Flower stalk withered — Dead leaves — Stem — Roots shrivel

Flowers

Herbaceous (leafy) perennials include members of the lily and iris families. Common lilies are tulips, hyacinths, onions, garlic and true lilies. Hyacinths are noted for their densely packed heads of scented flowers, and the tiger lily of China for its many varieties with large showy flowers much liked by gardeners. Waterlilies, which are unrelated, produce a thick rhizome form that gives rise to long stalks bearing leaves or flowers that usually lie flat on the surface of the water. The iris family is notable for spectacular flowers. In many species the flowers have equal numbers of upright and drooping petals. Irises include the common crocus and freesias.

Tulips are typical early spring flowers.

Waterlily flowers stick up out of the water.

Life history

Strawberries are perennial clump-forming plants that reproduce asexually – not by forming underground storage organs, but by developing trailing stems, or runners. A new strawberry plant, in its first year, produces a cluster of leaves, flowers, fruits and runners. The following year some of the seeds may germinate and the runners will put down roots and eventually produce new plants. This continues year after year. The strawberries people eat are in fact swollen red fruit stalks; the true fruits are the tiny pips embedded in the surface.

Parent plant

New plant

Seed germinates

Runner (horizontal stem)

New plant growing from bud

YEAR ONE

YEAR TWO

YEAR THREE

HERBACEOUS PLANTS (Temperate)

Most species are dicotyledons (having two seed leaves). They include the cabbage family such as mustard, radish, turnip, cauliflower and broccoli, and the goosefoot family, for example, spinach and beet. Pansies, marigolds and petunias are typical garden flower species.

In autumn, the aerial parts of herbaceous plants – the stems, leaves and flower stalks – generally die down. Annual species have only one growing season, at the end of which the whole plant dies. Biennials complete their life cycles in two growing seasons. Herbaceous plants also include perennials such as irises. All three types are successful plants because they can grow from seed to flower in sometimes only a few weeks, spreading more rapidly than trees and shrubs that may grow for many years before flowering. However, gardeners in temperate climates regard species such as marigolds as half-hardy, because their seeds cannot withstand frost when germinating.

Shape and form

Meadow species such as poppies grow to 1 m (39 inches) tall, producing branched stalks with deeply divided leaves and roundish showy flowers. Foxgloves grow to 1.5 m (5 feet). They have a single stem topped with a cluster of up to 80 flowers. Alpine plants are usually compact to combat cold windy conditions. Thin flat hairy leaves absorb the maximum amount of light and warmth.

A carpet of alpine plants

Long-stemmed meadow flowers

Surviving

A sudden frost or snowfall can kill the soft tissues of plants. Species such as the edelweiss have a waxy covering on the leaves that traps heat. The mountain crowfoot has a cell sap containing chemicals that act as an antifreeze. The winter leaf and flower buds of most temperate species are protected by thick, waxy scale leaves, to guard against cold.

Frost on nettle leaves

Life history

Annual plants, such as larkspur, fat hen, poppy and chickweed, flower and die in one year. Towards the end of their growing season the flowers make seeds. The seeds are dispersed and remain dormant until the following spring. Then they germinate and the new plants produce leaves and flowers to carry on the species. Biennial plants live for two years. They include wild carrot, cow parsley and cornflower. In the first year they produce only stems and leaves. In the second year they produce more leaves as well as flowers and seeds before dying. Species such as white campion grow as annuals or perennials.

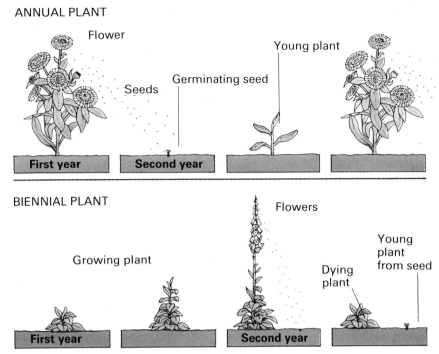

ANNUAL PLANT

Flower

Young plant

Seeds

Germinating seed

First year

Second year

BIENNIAL PLANT

Flowers

Growing plant

Young plant from seed

Dying plant

First year

Second year

Seed dispersal

The fruits or seeds of many plants are adapted to travel far from the parent plant to avoid overcrowding. The seeds of dandelions, thistles and clematis have feathery hairs that are caught by the wind. The parachute-like structures fall very slowly to the ground. The pods of peas, beans and lupins dry in the sun, shrivel then burst open to flick out the seeds. Fruits such as tomatoes, strawberries and blackberries are brightly colored and succulent to attract animals. Their fleshy tissues are swallowed and eaten, but the seeds inside the animal are not digested and pass out with the feces. Burdocks produce hooked fruits that catch in the fur of passing animals.

Dandelion
Relies on the wind for seed dispersal

Pea
Plants of the pea family produce pods that throw the seeds out

Tomato
Animals eat the fruit and disperse the seeds.

Burdock
Hook-like seeds attach themselves to animals for dipsersal

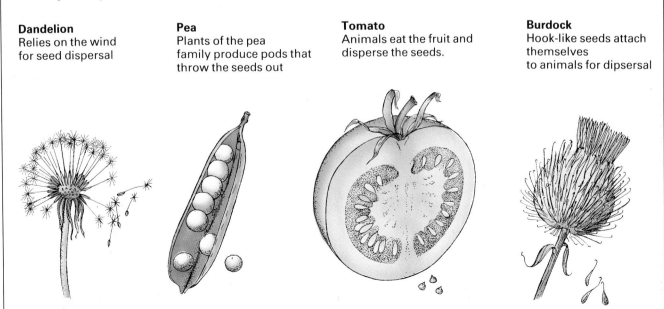

HERBACEOUS PLANTS (Tropical)

Major types:
Cacti are native to dry tropical North and South America and also include the prickly pear plants (opuntias). **Bromeliads** are native to South America. They have leaves that change color. **Orchids** include many species that live on trees. **Succulents** include the desert agaves and euphorbias, which grow to 30 m (100 feet).

In dry scrubland and in deserts, plants have to cope with a constant lack of water. Among adaptations to this, cacti, for example, have no leaves and photosynthesize in their green stems and branches. The lack of leaves prevents them losing the water formed in cell food production. Succulents are plants with thick water-retaining leaves and, like cacti, most have long roots, allowing them to reach water deep underground. In tropical rainforests, orchids and bromeliads grow on the branches of trees where they receive nutrients from rotting vegetation on the bark. The flowers are insect-pollinated and their seeds are usually dispersed by birds and other animals.

Surviving

Cactus is the Greek word for prickly plant, and many cacti bear spiny stems and fruits that deter animals from eating them. Bromeliads in the rainforest canopy produce roots that are used mainly for attaching the plant to its support. They obtain nutrients from the vase-like container of water and dissolved minerals formed by the circular clump, or rosette, of leaves. Some desert plants stop growing altogether when water supplies dry up. Their seeds germinate only when enough rain falls for them to produce leaves, flowers and fruits before the ground dries again. Similar adaptations in plants of dry grasslands, such as the African savannah, transform a barren landscape into a sea of flowers as soon as rains start.

Saguaro cactus in the Arizona Desert

A bromeliad clings to another plant for support.

Gourd seed pods wait for rain in the Sahara.

Feeding

The most remarkable feeding habits of plants are found among the pitcher plants. They have enlarged leaves fused together to form a trap for flies, ants and beetles. The jungles of India and Australasia have plants with a cup-shaped pitcher up to 30 cm (12 inches) deep and containing 2 liters (3.4 pints) of water. Insects are attracted to the pitcher by smell, color and a sugary fluid around the rim. As they enter they lose their footing, fall into the water and drown. Glands at the base of the pitcher produce chemicals that digest the animal food to provide essential minerals for the plant.

An Asian pitcher plant traps insects for food.

Flowers

The largest flower in the world is that of the rafflesia plant of Malaysia. The plant, which has no proper stem or leaves, grows on the branches of a vine tree absorbing water and nutrients from the host. The flower grows to 1 m (39 inches) across but lasts only a week. Orchids produce flowers with a lip that has a distinctive color or shape to attract insects or even small birds for pollination. In bee orchids, the lip resembles a female bee and males visit the flowers expecting to mate. The banana family includes the bird of paradise and ginger plants. Several South American plants have flowers pollinated by hummingbirds which, with their thin beaks and long tongues, are the only animals able to reach the nectar at the base.

The agave is pollinated by hummingbirds.

GRASSES

Major types:
Cereals have spikelets of flowers producing edible seeds. The major species are wheat, rice, maize (corn), barley, rye, oat, sorghum and millet. **Bamboos** are tropical woody species. **Reeds, rushes, sedges, bulrushes and reed-maces** are moisture-loving grasses mostly of tropical regions.

There are nearly 10,000 species of grasses and the related reeds and rushes. They form one of the largest families of flowering plants and are the most important economically. Either as cereals or as forage for farm animals, they are the main source of food for most people in the world. All are monocotyledons (having a single seed-leaf) with ribbon-like leaves, upright stems and thread-like roots. The flowers are tiny and are often clustered together in units called spikelets. They can rapidly colonize waste land. Among cereals, wheat is the major species of temperate regions, rice of tropical Asia and Africa, and maize, or corn, of tropical South America.

Structure and form

The stems of grasses are usually circular and hollow, and they bear long narrow leaves. The lower part of each leaf is wrapped around the stem. Underground, buds develop into new side-shoots to form a clump of stems, and many species spread like weeds by producing rhizomes or runners each with several growing points. Flowers develop at the top of stems in groups known as spikelets. They are adapted for wind pollination. They usually lack petals and sepals and have feathery stigmas and large anthers that hang outside the protective bracts so that wind shakes the pollen free.

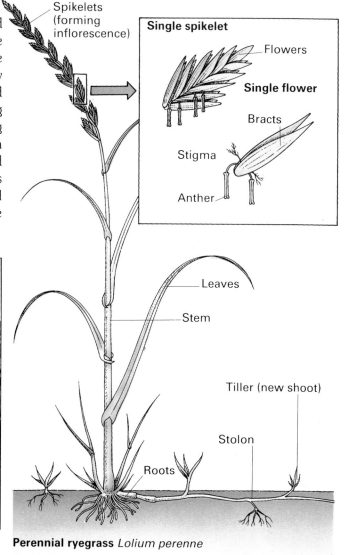

Spikelets (forming inflorescence)

Single spikelet

Flowers

Single flower

Bracts

Stigma

Anther

Leaves

Stem

Tiller (new shoot)

Stolon

Roots

Perennial ryegrass *Lolium perenne*

Tufts of bunch grass in the Andes Mountains

Seeds

The seeds of cereal grasses can be quite large, as in maize (corn), and contain large amounts of nutritious carbohydrates, or sugars. Rice and maize, for example, are the staple diets of many countries. Barley grains are a source of malt used for brewing, and wheat provides flour for making bread and pasta. The flower head is often called an ear and the individual seeds, grains. Winnowing is the removal of the grains from the rest of the ear, the chaff, by wind or air currents. Modern cereals are the result of thousands of years of selection and breeding to produce crops that will grow in almost any given climate and which will be resistant to pests.

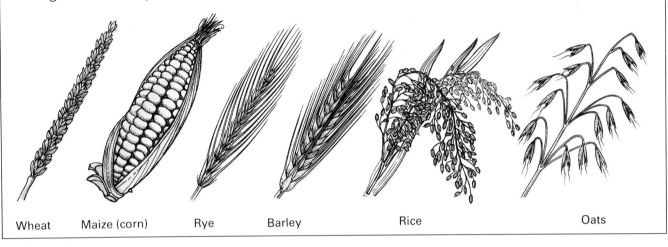

| Wheat | Maize (corn) | Rye | Barley | Rice | Oats |

Habitats

Grasses are extremely common and widely distributed, and grow in temperate chalkland areas, in tropical swamps and rainforests, in desert and on high mountains. The so-called grasslands of the world include the steppes of central Asia, the prairies of North America and the savannahs of Africa. Bamboos grow mostly in tropical regions and, as in parts of Southeast Asia, often form dense forests. Their stems grow to 30 m (100 ft) high and 50 cm (20 inches) in diameter. They bear leaves all the way up, but as the bamboo gets older, leaves drop from the lower part of the stem. Reeds grow along ditches, ponds and lakes. Rushes colonize bogs and marshes in all parts of the world except the tropics.

Reeds fringing a lake in southern France

Giant bamboos growing in Sri Lanka

Flowering plants chart

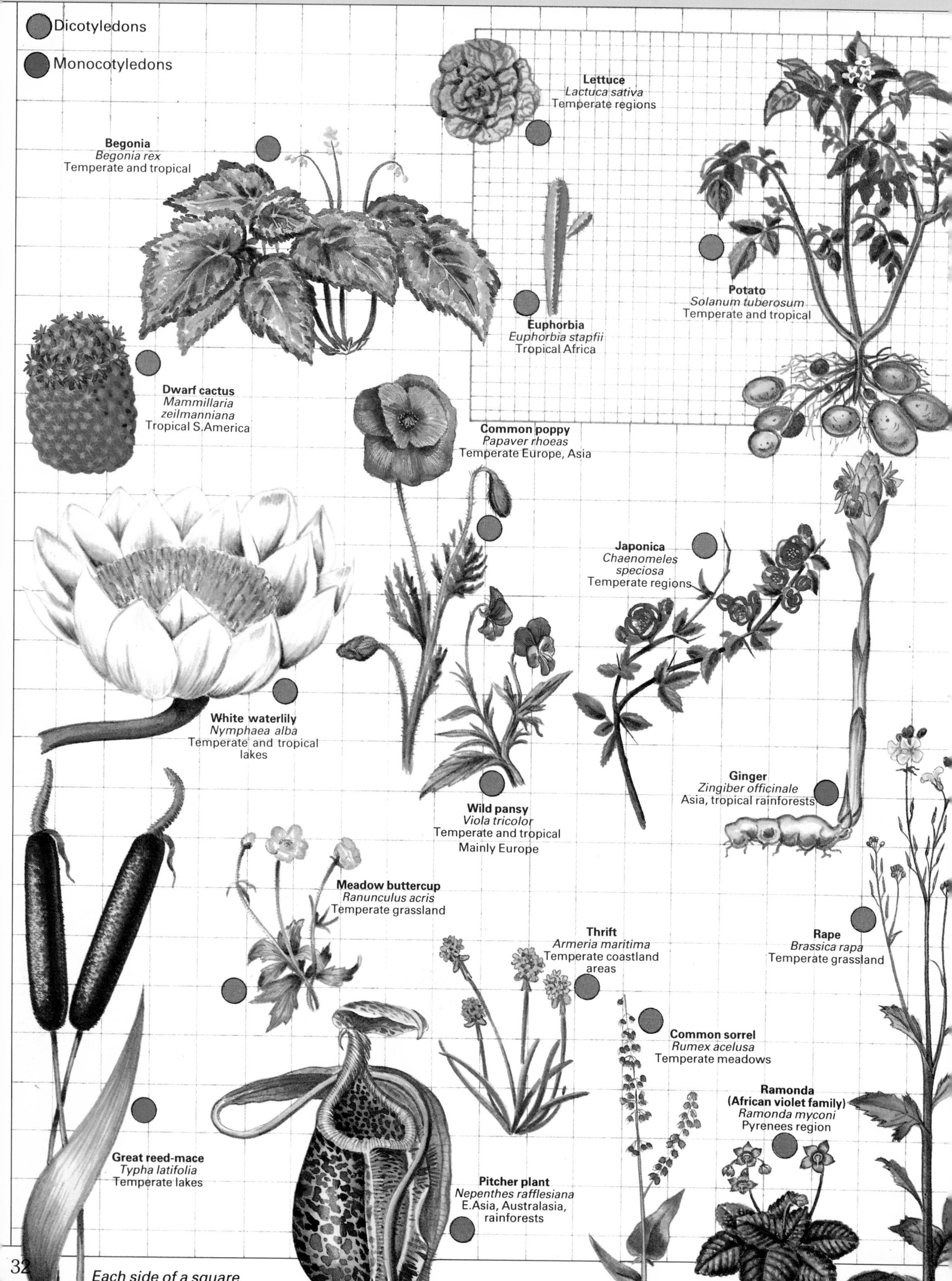

● Dicotyledons

● Monocotyledons

Lettuce
Lactuca sativa
Temperate regions

Begonia
Begonia rex
Temperate and tropical

Potato
Solanum tuberosum
Temperate and tropical

Dwarf cactus
*Mammillaria
zeilmanniana*
Tropical S.America

Euphorbia
Euphorbia stapfii
Tropical Africa

Common poppy
Papaver rhoeas
Temperate Europe, Asia

Japonica
*Chaenomeles
speciosa*
Temperate regions

White waterlily
Nymphaea alba
Temperate and tropical
lakes

Ginger
Zingiber officinale
Asia, tropical rainforests

Wild pansy
Viola tricolor
Temperate and tropical
Mainly Europe

Meadow buttercup
Ranunculus acris
Temperate grassland

Thrift
Armeria maritima
Temperate coastland
areas

Rape
Brassica rapa
Temperate grassland

Common sorrel
Rumex acelusa
Temperate meadows

**Ramonda
(African violet family)**
Ramonda myconi
Pyrenees region

Great reed-mace
Typha latifolia
Temperate lakes

Pitcher plant
Nepenthes rafflesiana
E.Asia, Australasia,
rainforests

32

*Each side of a square
represents 3 cm (1.2 in)*

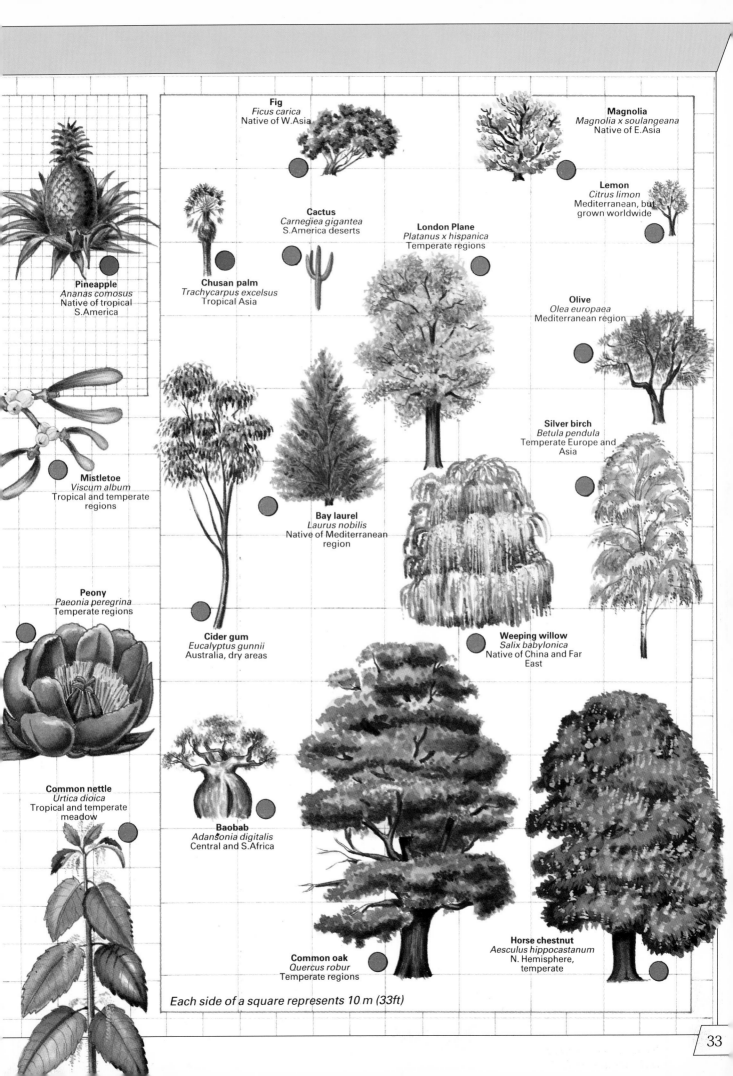

Fig
Ficus carica
Native of W.Asia

Magnolia
Magnolia x soulangeana
Native of E.Asia

Cactus
Carnegiea gigantea
S.America deserts

Lemon
Citrus limon
Mediterranean, but
grown worldwide

London Plane
Platanus x hispanica
Temperate regions

Chusan palm
Trachycarpus excelsus
Tropical Asia

Olive
Olea europaea
Mediterranean region

Pineapple
Ananas comosus
Native of tropical
S.America

Silver birch
Betula pendula
Temperate Europe and
Asia

Mistletoe
Viscum album
Tropical and temperate
regions

Bay laurel
Laurus nobilis
Native of Mediterranean
region

Weeping willow
Salix babylonica
Native of China and Far
East

Peony
Paeonia peregrina
Temperate regions

Cider gum
Eucalyptus gunnii
Australia, dry areas

Common nettle
Urtica dioica
Tropical and temperate
meadow

Baobab
Adansonia digitalis
Central and S.Africa

Horse chestnut
Aesculus hippocastanum
N. Hemisphere,
temperate

Common oak
Quercus robur
Temperate regions

Each side of a square represents 10 m (33ft)

33

The variety of living things is enormous. Plants, for example, range from microscopic mosses to conifer trees growing 100m (330ft) tall. Yet all plants photosynthesize and, in terms of internal structure and methods of reproduction, can be grouped into just four main sub-divisions. The most primitive plants are the Bryophytes. These lack true roots, stems or leaves. The next sub-division, the Pteridophytes, includes plants with roots, stems and leaves but which depend on water for their sexual reproduction. Third are the Gymnosperms, the cone-forming plants, and last, the Angiosperms, the flowering plants.

Algae, fungi, lichens and bacteria are often treated as simple types of plants. They each have one or more plant characteristics. In the main part of the book this treatment is maintained to highlight the probable course of evolution of today's plants. It shows that the first plants were probably single-celled aquatic organisms and what adaptations were needed to become large, land-living organisms such as conifer trees. Biologists, though, now often classify these organisms separately. Viruses are considered by some scientists as non-living things and by others as living, so are kept separate.

PLANT KINGDOM

Gymnosperms	Bryophytes	Pteridophytes	Angiosperms		
			Monocotyledons		Dicotyledons

Conifers

Mosses

Horsetails

Palms Grasses

Broadleaf trees

Ginkgoes

Clubmosses

Liverworts

Ferns

Orchids Lilies

Shrubs

Yews

Irises Bamboos

Herbaceous plants

ORGANISMS SOMETIMES CLASSED AS PLANTS

Algae	Bacteria	Lichens	Fungi

Euglena Spirogyra

Bacteria

Lichens

Molds Yeasts

VIRUSES

Plant plankton Seaweed

Puffballs Toadstools

GLOSSARY

adaptation a feature or pattern of growth that allows a plant to live in a particular environment

algae simple plants or plant-like photosynthesizing organisms consisting of either a single cell or many cells not organized into leaves, stems and roots

anther the male part of a flower, which produces pollen

antheridium the male reproductive organ of lower plants

aquatic an animal or plant which lives in water

archegonium the female reproductive organ of lower plants

asexual reproduction production of new plants not involving reproductive cells, or gametes. Includes binary fission, vegetative propagation

bacteria single-celled plant-like organisms, some of which cause diseases of animals and plants, others the decomposition of dead organisms

binary fission a method of asexual reproduction among some single-celled organisms involving division of the cell into two identical daughter cells

bract a leaf on a flower stalk specialized to protect a flower

cambium a layer of actively growing cells inside a stem

cell the building block of all living creatures. Different types of cells have different jobs – for example, xylem, phloem and epidermis cells – but all work in the same way

chlorophyll a green pigment inside plant cells that can trap sunlight and use its energy to make simple chemicals into complex energy-storing ones

cotyledon a specialized, food-storing leaf within a seed

disperse to spread spores or seeds away from the parent plant to prevent overcrowding

dormant period a time during which a plant rests and makes little or no new growth

egg female reproductive cell with its own provision of food for the growing embryo. The egg must be fertilized by the male sperm before development of the embryo can begin

embryo a stage in development of a new plant – from the fertilized egg until the young plant germinates

epidermis a protective layer of cells on the outside of a leaf or stem

fertilization the fusing together of male and female reproductive cells (sperm and egg, or pollen grain and egg within ovule) to form a young plant or embryo

frond the leaf-like structure of large algae such as seaweeds or the usually finely divided leaves of ferns

fungi organisms with some plant-like features but that do not photosynthesize

gamete a reproductive cell such as a sperm or egg. Sexual reproduction involves fertilization, the fusion of male and female gametes

gametophyte a stage in the life cycle of plants which produces gametes

germination the sprouting of a new plant from a seed or spore

habitat a place where an animal or plant lives

host a creature on or in which a parasite lives

nucleus the control center of a cell

organ major part of a plant which has a specific job, for instance a leaf, stem or root

organism a living thing such as an animal or plant

ovule part of a flower containing the female gamete that will develop into a seed

ovum an unfertilized egg

parasite a creature that lives in or on another creature from which it gets its food (the host). A parasite may eventually kill its food source

photosynthesis the production of food by green plants from carbon dioxide and water using sunlight as energy

pollen the male gametes of flowering plants

sexual reproduction production of new plants by the fusion of male and female gametes, either sperm and egg or pollen grain and egg within an ovule

species animals or plants that have the same structure

spore an asexual reproductive or resting structure from which new individuals develop

sporophyte a stage in the life cycle of plants that produces spores

vascular system the water-conducting vessels and food-transporting sieve tubes within more advanced plants such as ferns, conifers and flowering plants

INDEX

All entries in bold are found in the Glossary

Photographic Credits
(l=left, r=right, t=top, b=bottom, c=center)
Cover, contents page, pages 6 (t), 8, 9 (l and r), 11 (all), 17 (both), 20 (both), 23 (tl, tr and bl), 26 (all) and back cover: Bruce Colman; pages 6 (l), 25 (r), 28 (r) and 31 (r): Robert Harding; pages 6 (r), 12, 28 (t) and 31 (t): John Lythgoe/Planet Earth; page 7 (t): Leo Collier/Planet Earth; pages 7 (b), 9 (b), 16 (r), 28 (l) and 30: Ardea; pages 16 (l), 21 (r) and 29 (t): Frank Lane Agency; page 21 (l): Cameron Read/Planet Earth; page 22: Jorge Provenza/Planet Earth; page 23 (br): Richard Coomber/Planet Earth; pages 25 (l) and 29 (b): Ivor Edmond/Planet Earth.